LIFE SOURCE

6 GUARDRAILS TO EXPERIENCE FEWER REGRETS, LIVE SKILLFULLY, AND MAKE BETTER DECISIONS

LIFE SOURCE

6 GUARDRAILS TO EXPERIENCE FEWER REGRETS, LIVE SKILLFULLY, AND MAKE BETTER DECISIONS

JEFF HUSTON & GABE OLSON

Life Source by Jeff Huston and Gabe Olson © 2024
Wildly Wise, LLC. All rights reserved.

Printed in the United States of America

Published by Ethos Collective™
PO Box 43, Powell, OH 43065
EthosCollective.vip

This book contains material protected under international and federal copyright laws and treaties. Any unauthorized reprint or use of this material is prohibited. No part of this book may be reproduced or transmitted in any form or by any means, electronic or mechanical, including photocopying, recording, or by any information storage and retrieval system, without express written permission from the author.

LCCN: 2024914870
Paperback ISBN: 978-1-63680-347-0
Hardcover ISBN: 978-1-63680-348-7
e-book ISBN: 978-1-63680-349-4

Available in paperback, hardcover, e-book, and audiobook.

All Scripture quotations, unless otherwise indicated, are taken from the Holy Bible, New International Version, NIV. Copyright © 1973, 1978, 1984 by Biblica, Inc.™ Used by permission of Zondervan. All rights reserved worldwide.

Any Internet addresses (websites, blogs, etc.) and telephone numbers printed in this book are offered as a resource. They are not intended in any way to be or imply an endorsement by Ethos Collective™, nor does Ethos Collective™ vouch for the content of these sites and numbers for the life of this book.

Some names and identifying details may have been changed to protect the privacy of individuals.

ACKNOWLEDGMENTS

When thinking through the long list of people and life experiences on this journey, first and foremost on the list is our Savior, whose grace and sacrifice saved us and are more than sufficient for us every day.

We are grateful for our wives and families who direct, teach, and model love—inspiring us to be better and more than we believe we are capable of moment by moment. To the team around us in so many different areas and ventures.

Our story is inspired by the life lessons we learn every day and the growth that GRACIE demands of us, calling us to be better together than apart.

TABLE OF CONTENTS

INTRODUCTION 1
THE ALLURE OF GRACIE 7
GRACIE AS A CATALYST 13
GUARD YOUR HEART 17
GRATITUDE 23
RESULTS 31
ACCOUNTABILITY 37
COMMUNICATION 49
INTEGRITY 61
ENERGY 71
CLOSING 83
RECOMMENDED READING AND
OTHER RESOURCES 87
ABOUT THE AUTHORS 91
    JEFF HUSTON 91
    GABE OLSON 92

INTRODUCTION

I'd like to introduce you to someone who has become one of the most important people in my life. Her name is GRACIE, and next to my relationship with my Creator and my wife, GRACIE is the most important person to me. That's a significant and powerful thing to say because it means I'm saying that GRACIE is more important than my relationship with my kids and grandkids, more important than my relationship with my parents or my siblings, more important than any other significant relationship in my life.

GRACIE has changed my life, and I believe she can change yours too.

The first time I told my wife I wanted to introduce her to someone who had become very significant in my life, she got very defensive. However, after getting to know GRACIE, she fell in love with her and has come to respect her as much as I do.

So, who is GRACIE, and how did she come to be? She is the life source, the inspiration for the title of the book. That's what this book is about. But before we dive into the details, I'd like to give you the backstory, which begins with someone well-known in history.

King Solomon has always been a very fascinating story to me. From the time I was a small boy, going to church and Bible classes, I heard many stories about the fame and adventures of King Solomon. But when I was twelve, I read a part of the story that captivated me and forever impacted my life.

Solomon was quite young when he became king. Many biblical scholars believe that he was between twenty and twenty-two years of age, but some argue that he was as young as fifteen. In any case, he was very young and certainly lacked the experience he would need to lead the country—especially when you consider that he was taking over for his father, King David, whose reign and conquests were well documented. As the story goes, shortly after being crowned king, God visited Solomon in a dream and told him that he (God) would give him anything he asked for.

Just imagine that! The God of the universe comes to you and says that he will grant you anything you want. It's like the proverbial genie in a bottle, and he wants to grant you three wishes. As a twelve-year-old boy, I couldn't believe what I was reading! Why would a young man, possibly as little as three years older than I was when I was reading the story, ask for what Solomon asked for? It didn't make any sense to me.

As the story goes, Solomon asked God for wisdom instead of all the other things he could have thought of. If that had been me, I would have thought of a hundred other things to ask for rather than that. Who would have blamed him if he had asked for peace in his kingdom, prosperity, or a long life for himself? What would have to be inside of a person at such a young age (or any age, for that matter) to even think of asking for wisdom?

We must remember that the Bible isn't the only history book that mentions King Solomon. Several non-Biblical accounts of King Solomon record him as a real person and that he had an unusual amount of wisdom and intelligence. The Bible unpacks that further and says he was unique in human history. In 1 Kings 3:12, God tells him, "I have given you a wise and understanding heart, so that there has not been anyone like you before you, nor shall any like you arise after you." So, there had never been anyone as wise as Solomon, and there would never be anyone as wise as him in the future. He is unequaled in human history, which, if you think about it, is pretty amazing!

We all want our lives to matter, and most of us have a desire within us to be significant. We attempt to live our lives in a way that our existence has meaning. We want to have an impact and be a part of something bigger than ourselves. Obviously, few of us accomplish that. A hundred years after you or I die, who will remember us? I'm at peace with that reality because I know that there is an eternal story that goes beyond my lifetime. But when history tells us that Solomon was unique, it's saying something.

History records some 3,000 proverbs and wise sayings credited to him, so Solomon had much to say about life. All this background sets the stage for the importance of what he says in Proverbs 4:23. "Above all else," Let's pause there for a moment. Solomon has an incredible amount of accumulated knowledge, information, experience, and understanding that is unique in human history, and he starts this thought with the words "Above all else." In other words, he's about to say the most important thing, what he considers more significant than anything he's ever said or thought. Coming from the guy who's unique in human history, we should be on the edge of our seats!

We often miss the significance of who Solomon was: who history says that he was and who the Bible says he was. For him to make the statement, "Above all else, guard your heart for it determines the direction of your life," it should stop us in our tracks.

Our hearts are the wellspring of our lives. It can be a source of life when protected but also our most vulnerable weakness if left unguarded.

The question we should all be asking at this point is: How do we guard our hearts? If it's that important, what are the criteria? What are the guardrails that I should have around me, around my life, to guard my heart, my life source, so I can experience the wisdom, freedom, and peace that comes with living a fulfilled life?

Her value exceeds pearls; all you desire can't compare with her.
— Proverbs 3:15

CHAPTER ONE

THE ALLURE OF GRACIE

Have you ever loved someone who makes you want to be a better person? If yes, you know the kind of love I'm talking about. Loved in a way that's both soft and strong, providing comfort and challenges while soothing you with their presence and inspiring you to reach new heights. Love that motivates you with its being, the things love stands for, and the way love touches your heart. Being in love is like a spark of joy that moves you—all the while, love accepts you as you are and has no requirement for you to change. Yet, you feel so elevated, encouraged, and exhilarated you can't help but grow and advance your goals. Being in a relationship with that kind of love causes a response in you to succeed at a higher level and become the best version of yourself.

That's the power of GRACIE. When committed to love and wisdom, what GRACIE is, you live with **purpose**,

authenticity, and a sense of **fulfillment**. Every moment with her is a new opportunity to choose improvement over stagnancy. She helps you realize your potential, transform your life, and experience freedom like you've never experienced before.

The truth is much of the world lives in contrast to this. Living in a way that comes across as a very selfish, mundane, and stagnant life, with each person out to get what they can out of every experience. They rush from one appointment to the next, hustling for dollars and taking advantage of people and policies without attention, thought, or care. They're stuck in a rut, wondering if life is a racetrack of working, paying bills, and keeping up with the Joneses. Relationships for this group come after materialism, and they're unfulfilling at best. Most people live completely unaware that there's an untapped source of abundance filled with endless opportunities and unforeseen paths—if only they'd commit to something.

They have no idea how to create success and contentment, be genuine, and serve the people they encounter. As a result of this disconnect, they often feel alone, struggling with an elusive pull, wondering, "Surely, there's more to life than this."

We're here to tell you there is, and it begins with a wholehearted commitment to GRACIE.

GRACIE is the most important person in my life.

GRACIE is the perfect model for every person who wants to grow and help others succeed with them.

GRACIE is not my wife. She's my model, my mindset, and my way of life.

GRACIE is for me, and GRACIE is for you.

GRACIE is an acronym for six principles that can help create a society of successful, selfless, and genuine individuals more aware of the world, events, and people around them.

The acronym stands for:

G - Gratitude
R - Results
A - Accountability
C - Communication
I - Integrity
E - Energy

Following is a brief overview of each of the principles we'll cover throughout this book to help you unlock your potential, experience a life transformation, and live with the greatest sense of freedom while traversing life arm-in-arm with the beloved GRACIE.

Gratitude is the key to unlocking abundance. When we live with a spirit of gratitude, we can appreciate the beauty and blessings around us. We open our hearts to the possibilities ahead of us through gratitude.

Results is about being intentional and focusing on action, self-reflection, and growth. Pursuing our goals and aspirations allows us to discover the depth of our potential and realize those results, only to use them to fuel further progress. By committing ourselves, we can witness the transformation of our dreams into actual reality.

Accountability is a reminder that we are accountable to God as the director of our path. When we ask for His direction and take ownership of our actions, decisions, and consequences, His provision and guidance lead the way. Through this mutual respect and submission, we are led to live a life of purpose and fulfillment. We become architects of our lives when we take ownership of our actions, decisions, and consequences. By embracing accountability, we free ourselves from victimhood and empower ourselves to live a future of purpose and fulfillment.

Communication is about fostering authentic connections and nurturing relationships. We bridge the many social, cultural, or linguistic gaps that separate us from others through open dialogue and respect for those we communicate with, helping to build understanding and empathy. The art of effective communication can help us inspire, motivate, and uplift those around us.

Integrity refers to the moral compass that guides our actions and begins with self-leadership. When we operate with integrity, and our moral compass leads our actions, we align our thoughts, words, and deeds. By staying true to our values and upholding certain ethical principles, we can also help inspire others.

Energy is the life force that permeates our very being. It propels us with enthusiasm. We all have unique energy levels, but tapping into and harnessing that inner spark fuels the journey.

We believe unlocking the power of GRACIE means embarking on a path of limitless possibilities. Though the acronym is something we crafted, we believe these six principles represent timeless ideas and concepts. A commitment to GRACIE yields the essence of a good life—a life that isn't of value just to you, but also to those around you.

In short, this book aims to provide you with a well-rounded grasp of the transformative principles behind GRACIE while offering practical guidance and insight into some of the experiences that shaped our understanding of these principles.

By exploring GRACIE and our commitment to the principles, we aim to help you address every aspect of the six principles of GRACIE: Gratitude, Results, Accountability, Communication, Integrity, and Energy. We'll peel back the layers, sharing stories, examples, and practical steps that will act as your guide toward long-term success. Together, we'll delve into each principle, exploring its essence and equipping you with the tools to thrive through personal transformation and actualizing your potential so you can live freely and abundantly.

*Make the path of your feet level.
Let all of your ways be established.*
—Proverbs 4:26

CHAPTER TWO

GRACIE AS A CATALYST

GRACIE represents everything beautiful in this world, and she wants us to experience everything beautiful as well. Her mindset is loving, accepting, and full of wisdom. Embracing GRACIE as a catalyst to that beautiful life is a mindset that can serve you.

GRACIE is a lens through which to view the world and approach every aspect of your life. Though it is a set of principles, it is more than the sum of its parts; it's a way of being that can redefine our thoughts, actions, and interactions with others. The GRACIE mindset allows us to harmonize with the various parts of life.

Once engaged with GRACIE, those who commit to her will:

- Cultivate a sense of gratitude, finding joy in the simplest of moments.
- Learn to use results not as an end but as a tool.
- Own our choices and the ethical principles we believe in.
- Understand the value of engaging in open, empathetic, and, above all, authentic dialogue with others.
- Grow interested in creating a better world around ourselves.
- Deny periods of stagnancy, choosing progress, growth, and motivation.

By simply committing to GRACIE's principles, she inspires us to make the right choices consistently. She's the voice in our heads telling us to take a moment, think things through, and consider the options. GRACIE helps us gain clarity amid all the options around us. She inspires us to play the long game, think about the result of each choice, and determine the best course of action to align with our long-term goals. GRACIE helps us think big. She ensures that we weigh all potential outcomes and imagine not just how they'll impact us but those around us.

Being true to GRACIE helps us live with purpose, authenticity, and fulfillment.

GRACIE inspires us to live according to biblical principles, tap into our innate potential, and rely on God's promises

Life Source

to create the life we want for ourselves. She reminds us that our lives are not just random events but deeply purposeful steps connected to God's glory and full of meaning. She reminds us we are here for a purpose while offering growth, contribution, and self-discovery opportunities.

A commitment to GRACIE helps us build the resilience and adaptability we need to navigate the ups and downs of life. When things go wrong, she's there to comfort us and help us view setbacks and challenges as valuable learning opportunities rather than roadblocks. With GRACIE as a guide, we develop the ability to bounce back from adversity, embrace change, and find creative solutions to overcome the obstacles that come our way.

Those committed to GRACIE demonstrate how to build deep connections and meaningful relationships built on the utmost trust, respect, and compassion. When we follow the principles of GRACIE, we build trust and earn respect from others. GRACIE's beloveds can make a genuine, positive impact in their communities and beyond through sustainable relationships.

Although it can be vulnerable to put your heart, your life source, into the world and build fruitful relationships, GRACIE helps you protect your heart.

*Above all else, guard your heart,
for it is the wellspring of life.*
—Proverbs 4:23

CHAPTER THREE

GUARD YOUR HEART

If you had a wellspring that was your sole source of joy, power, and will, you'd go to great lengths to shield and protect it above all else. Your heart is that wellspring, and as the center of your being, it directs everything you do and defines how you show up. Paying attention to your heart's messages, observing its feelings, and obeying its convictions is essential.

The heart is the root of all joy but can lead to suffering if compromised. We live in a world where the challenges and temptations around us make us vulnerable, and GRACIE is protection against such vulnerabilities. When we live life in concert with GRACIE, we take active measures to protect the core of our being. She is our shield when temptations and hardships relentlessly attack the walls of our hearts.

An unguarded heart is divided and open to doubt and distress. Despite the turbulences of life, a guarded heart is protected and rests in peace. Rather than pouring from an empty cup or feeling depleted, a guarded heart honors dependence upon God. In each moment of emptiness, it seeks Him for replenishment. A guarded heart is attuned to God, faithful to His word, and purposeful in every action and reaction. A heart with this orientation is well cared for and abundant, providing the ability to refill, refresh, pour into, and serve others. Those with guarded hearts are internally sourced by God and have the abundance and depth of character to impact those who are hurting and in situations, even the most unjust situations, where they need to be uplifted.

By obeying His Father's will with unflinching, extraordinary, and resolute devotion, Jesus showed us the perfect example of living with a guarded heart. Despite the betrayal, mocking, intense beatings, and crucifixion, Jesus prayed. Though weary, he loved and commanded peace, followed the scriptures, and requested forgiveness for others when he cried out from the cross, "Father, forgive them, for they know not what they do" (Luke 23:34).

In the following chapters, we'll take a closer look at how Jesus sets the example of a guarded heart and walk through each component of GRACIE with a related bible verse. For now, let's talk about how GRACIE equips us to guard our hearts to have a singular vision and commitment like Jesus. Through this vision and dedication, we can ensure that our commitment and the wellspring that flows from our hearts are uncontaminated. Learning to guard your heart and protect your vision is a journey of self-discovery and personal growth. Along the way, we learn, adapt, and walk the path

Life Source

God lays out for us with the strength and commitment Jesus demonstrated.

With GRACIE as a guardrail, we are shielded and supported in our most challenging times, provided we choose to let her in.

But how exactly does GRACIE guide us to guard our hearts?

It's because GRACIE is a *guardrail*, a railing along a hazardous edge. GRACIE makes our health, happiness, and fulfillment her priority. When we abide by GRACIE's caring, nurturing, and loving presence like we would heed a barrier on the border of a mountain trail, she keeps us on the right path and stops us from slipping into the hazard.

Not only do they keep us out of harm's way, but guardrails help us live more authentically by:

- Shielding us from harmful and toxic influences.
- Helping us establish healthy boundaries and avoid situations that may compromise our emotional well-being.
- Cultivating and maintaining healthy relationships.
- Fostering open communication, trust, and mutual respect.
- Preventing emotional manipulation.
- Ensuring our values are honored.
- Nurturing relationships based on genuine connection and support.

Life is filled with no shortage of ups and downs—without emotional guardrails, our hearts may become vulnerable. But with GRACIE, we can navigate life's challenges with greater equilibrium. Guardrails allow us to process emotions healthily and maintain stability in our relationships and personal lives.

As a guardrail herself, GRACIE is dedicated to upholding you; she is there in the brightest and darkest hour, and her gift is that of love: boundless, selfless love. And ultimately, love can save every soul.

With warmth and compassion, GRACIE encourages us to reflect on our values, beliefs, and aspirations. Above all else, when adhering and devoting to God's direction and guidance, the principles of GRACIE offer a guardrail to ensure your heart's wellspring is abundant, free flowing, and protected from unexpected compromise.

Rejoice always, pray continually, and give thanks in all circumstances; for this is God's will for you in Christ Jesus.
—1 Thessalonians 5:18

CHAPTER FOUR

GRATITUDE

Regardless of the great trials Jesus experienced, he remained present, connected to, and responsive to God's will for his life. A play on words reveals the truth of this verse. It's about being grateful **in** the experience, not necessarily grateful **for** the experience. During the most trying circumstances and situations anyone would find challenging to be grateful for, Jesus chose the condition of his heart. His choice was gratitude, knowing everything was working together for good.

When you give thanks, you are choosing the best of ways. Life is a choice; we can choose to be ungrateful and morose, always complaining or looking for an outlet for our problems—or, we can learn to take things as they are and be grateful for what matters.

The first letter of GRACIE, G for *Gratitude*, as exemplified by Jesus, is not a passive response; it's an active choice. It is a state of being that looks beyond the external circumstances and into the depths of our hearts. When we cultivate gratitude, we *shift our perspective*, finding blessings despite adversity. *Whatever we think about continually, we create in our lives.*

Being Grateful IN

Just as Jesus taught us, gratitude is not meant to diminish the pain or difficulties we may face but to remind us that even in the darkest moments, there is still light to be found.

When faced with trials and challenges, we may wonder if there is a deeper purpose behind our suffering. But just because we experience a challenge **does not** necessarily mean that it is God's will for us to endure hardship. What truly matters is our perspective in the midst of these challenges. GRACIE teaches us to shift our focus from external to internal; she teaches us to find gratitude *within the experience* rather than being grateful for the experience itself. Jesus, too, was not grateful **for** his suffering but was grateful **in** it. Despite what he suffered, Jesus chose to see beyond the surface. James reminds us why we have joy and gratitude in suffering in James 1:2-4. "Consider it pure joy, my brothers and sisters, whenever you face trials of many kinds because you know that the testing of your faith produces perseverance. Let perseverance finish its work so that you may be mature and complete, not lacking anything."

Thus, a wiser choice is to focus less on the hardship and more on seeing the bigger picture that remains to be seen while remaining grateful *amidst* the situation. Particularly when there's hardship, there's another component of gratitude that's essential—that's being present. Presence is a state of focus when centered in the moment and mindful of every aspect of the here and now.

The 15-Minute Syndrome

Many individuals live in a perpetual state of anticipation, always looking toward the next moment or the next milestone. This "15-minute syndrome" manifests in a mindset that is forever 15 minutes ahead, preoccupied with what's on the horizon. They're always looking ahead to the next paycheck, planning the next meeting, stressing about the traffic on the ride home, or curious about how things will come together in the following days. More often than not, obsessive future focus overshadows the beauty of the *here and now*. Yet, the richness of our lives unfolds only in the present, and being present holds the key to gratitude.

To be more accurate, gratitude and presence are a chicken-and-egg situation—to be grateful is to be present and to be present is to be grateful. Each feeds into the next—begin with one, and you will naturally flow into the next. The more this cycle repeats, the more firmly one is rooted in the GRACIE framework.

The Gratitude Effect

The transformative power of gratitude extends beyond the immediate moment, influencing our mental health and shaping our relationships and mindset.

Gratitude can act as a balm, easing the stress on our minds. When we shift our focus from tomorrow's pressures to today's blessings, stress loses its stronghold. Furthermore, by acknowledging the positive aspects of our lives, even amidst challenges, gratitude offers a lifeline for those with anxiety and depression. Author, salesman, and motivational speaker Zig Ziglar goes a bit further, acknowledging gratitude as a **source** of well-being. He said, "The moment you begin to worry about the things you want and the things you don't have in life is the moment you will lose your gratitude… The greatest source of happiness is the ability to be grateful at all times."

Pausing, breathing, and being present in the moment naturally produce a gratitude response with a ripple effect; it creates a sustained sense of contentment that contributes to a happier and more fulfilling life. Gratitude is both an "in the moment" way of life and a practice. Have you heard of someone using a gratitude journal or jar to measure and track their gratitude process? Daily tracking is an effective way to shift the mind and improve outcomes in life.

A 2020 research study published in the Journal of Happiness Studies confirmed the impact of a 6-week gratitude intervention on mental health: "The sustained effects on mental well-being, appreciation of simple pleasure up to 6-months follow-up, suggest that it is possible to promote an appreciative and grateful perspective on life that becomes a lasting resource for living a resilient, joyful and meaningful life."[1]

---

[1] https://link.springer.com/article/10.1007/s10902-020-00261-5

Moreover, presence and gratitude not only enhance our individual well-being but also enrich our relationships. A study, *Beyond Reciprocity: Gratitude and Relationships in Everyday Life*, uncovered the role gratitude plays in connections with others, noting: "Relationships with others who are responsive to our whole self—our likes and dislikes, our needs and preferences—can help us get through difficult times and flourish in good times. Gratitude can be understood as an emotion that serves the social function of promoting such relationships."[2]

Creating a Habit Stack

Cultivating gratitude is like planting seeds in the garden of our lives; it takes time, care, and consistency. This is where habits come into play. When gratitude becomes a regular part of our routine, it becomes a natural response to life's moments. Simple habits like keeping a gratitude journal to jot down a few things you're thankful for each day or taking a moment to express thanks during meals can build a sturdy foundation for a fruitful gratitude practice.

Establishing gratitude as a practice is also where a *habit stack* is useful. A habit stack allows you to put your habits on autopilot, where one leads seamlessly into the next. Essentially, a habit stack is a physical or mnemonic reminder to stay present. A gratitude habit stack could be as simple as a gratitude rock you keep in your pocket or adding a printed Bible verse that resonates with you to your wallet or datebook. These reminders act as a gentle nudge in the right

---

[2] https://www.ncbi.nlm.nih.gov/pmc/articles/PMC2692821/

direction, reminding you to pause, be present, and be grateful in that moment. Through this practice and other positive habits, GRACIE becomes even more effective.

Going B.I.G

In conclusion, the most substantiative advice from GRACIE is this: start by going *B.I.G*, which stands for Beginning In Gratitude.

This first, incremental, daily practice can produce the biggest changes over time. Being grateful is a slight shift in mindset that has vital rewards. Because when we are grateful in every possibility, we are open to the second step of GRACIE—we learn how to process *Results*.

*A gracious woman gains respect,
but ruthless men gain only wealth.*
—Proverbs 11:16

CHAPTER FIVE

RESULTS

Blessed is the one who does not walk in step with the wicked or stand in the way that sinners take or sit in the company of mockers, but whose delight is in the law of the Lord, and who meditates on his law day and night.
That person is like a tree planted by streams of water, which yields its fruit in season and whose leaf does not wither—whatever they do prospers.
—Psalm 1:1-3

This passage in the Bible talks about the holiness and happiness of a godly man, describing the righteous as blessed, meaning they prosper in spirit. As one with a relationship with God, walking in His ways, with a heart that responds to Him, Jesus is the epitome of a righteous man. Jesus applied God's word with close application of mind and fixed thought.

When it came to results, Jesus understood that there were no unrealistic goals, only unrealistic timelines to achieve them. Regardless of what was happening around him or how "crazy" or outlandish his goal appeared to others, he was relentless in his pursuit. Jesus was unconcerned with the time it'd take to realize or experience the results of his quest but committed to the harvest that was sure to come.

Means and Ends

What Jesus understood was this: results are not the end goal. Instead, even results and goals are means, not the destination itself. They are like guideposts on the path of progress; they provide a concrete way of measuring growth, offering clarity and direction along our journeys. Jesus' goal was to show people the truth, but it was not his end. The truth was more like a tree planted in expectation for a future, accumulative harvest. We learn to adjust our course for better outcomes by understanding this structure of using results.

The truth Jesus knew, and the GRACIE framework encourages you to understand, is that in the pursuit of progress, the main result is progress itself. Rather than stagnating once we reach a desired result, it is better to return the fruit of the earth unto the earth and see the value in this toil. In this case, *the journey is the destination*, and each apparent end should be the means for further progress.

Progress, Not Perfection

With her presence, GRACIE provides a framework for our labor, but at the end of the day, she does not substitute it—there is no magical moment where all your goals are accomplished, and there is nothing more to do. While we often dream of such a state, imagine for a moment how stagnating it would be.

In truth, the goal is not an unattainable, idealized perfection. Perfection is a mirage, always shimmering in the distance but never within reach. Rather than striving for an impossible state of perfection, GRACIE urges us to focus on realistic, constructive progress. From the example of Jesus, we know that the key lies in making a positive choice, even in the face of overwhelming odds. Jesus did not rest upon his laurels at every high, or bemoan every low moment in his great and arduous journey. Instead, he maintained a positive, constructive attitude throughout, seeking not a perfect future state but *living in the present* and progressively improving what he could. The lesson to learn here is that while we might not be able to change our experiences, we can always change how we react to and perceive them.

The Results Economy

In the world around us exist two economies, and they are defined by how they react to the idea of results—these are the "Time and Effort Economy" versus the "Results Economy."

The former often stems from an entitlement mindset, expecting rewards for equivalent effort. The Time and Effort

Economy is mathematical, seemingly logical, and lacks vitality and space for extraordinary and otherworldly growth. The standard economy of effort is founded on the belief that results are *all that matter*—that goals are our ends. This economy is exemplified by an employee who clocks in their hours and demands compensation without ever trying to double down on their efforts or reinvest their reward into their position. The result is people stuck in passive ruts, unable to grow or progress. Traditional employment models foster a sense of entitlement from womb to tomb, and though each result is still a milestone, everything adds up to nothing because *no one is counting*.

On the contrary, the Results Economy operates in good faith. Those who abide by the Results Economy do two things: they Begin In Gratitude and understand that each achievement is only fuel to reach further heights. Just as Jesus used each achievement to facilitate his next aim, those who live by the Results Economy actively add value to their workplace, personal life, and other endeavors. This way of thinking is about treating effort and achievement in a non-transactional, selfless manner, understanding that good things come to those who *contribute value*.

When you show up at work or home, consider this: *how do I add value here?* It could mean putting in that little extra effort, doing that extra little something that elevates both you and everything around you. After all, this is what GRACIE does as well; she consistently *adds value* to your life by encouraging you to take ownership of it.

To understand the Results Economy is to know that you are responsible for yourself, your life, and your decisions—and if you know how to hold yourself accountable

Life Source

to them, you hold the ability to do something amazing with all three. Herein lies the key to the next component of GRACIE: *Accountability*.

*Be strong and courageous! Do not be afraid or discouraged.
For the Lord your God is with you wherever you go.*
—Joshua 1:9

CHAPTER SIX

ACCOUNTABILITY

As iron sharpens iron, so one person sharpens another.
—Proverbs 27:17

The actual process of creating an iron tool involves heating the substance until it becomes malleable and then beating it with an iron hammer to establish the edge. Through repeated heating, hammering, and cooling, a tool is formed. Once the tool is created, it's maintained and sharpened by being rubbed against another.

Your circle is comprised of men and women you'll rub against, which is why the people you surround yourself with matter. Individuals who are rooted in the word of God, choosing to make a difference in the world, and serving their communities will help you grow in your faith, challenge you to go further than you expected, and be available to support you when things don't go as planned. Dr. Henry Cloud, an acclaimed leadership expert, clinical psychologist, and New York Times bestselling Christian author, explains the value of being challenged to grow. He says, "As iron sharpens iron, we need confrontation and truth from others to grow. No one likes to hear negative things about him or herself. But in the long run, it may be good for us."

Accountability is crucial for personal and professional growth. It is not merely a buzzword; it is a vital concept that can transform the way individuals and teams operate. Accountability is not about pointing fingers or assigning blame but recognizing the interconnectedness of individuals within a shared framework.

Org Chart vs. Accountability Chart: A Paradigm Shift

When discussing accountability, it's important to look at how organizations are set up. The familiar organizational chart in most organizations dictates a top-down hierarchy, assigning levels and positions. Nonetheless, our collective perspective shifted when we were introduced to the accountability chart, courtesy of the Entrepreneurial Operating System (EOS) by Gino Wickman, author of the best-selling book, "Traction." This new approach, notably outlined in his book, led us down a transformative path, where Wickman explains the components essential to streamlining processes and improving business performance.

To fully comprehend the concept of the accountability chart and where this redirection took us, let's first discuss the disparities between the organization chart and the accountability chart.

Org charts function like a food chain, placing the owner or CEO at the top, with a descending hierarchy. This model can inadvertently foster a culture of hierarchy and a mindset that may not align with our values. The org chart, in essence, shapes how we perceive and value individuals within the organization. Unfortunately, these charts are superficial and don't serve as an exhaustive guide about individual roles or responsibilities within each team, making it difficult to hold the individuals accountable for their performance.

Reflecting on my own experiences, I recall a disconcerting encounter with someone in the real estate business who referred to tenants as "animals." His assertion sounded repulsive, to say the least. This incident reinforced my commitment to viewing people with respect and avoiding such dehumanizing perspectives. In my opinion, org charts perceive individuals in a somewhat similar, although not entirely identical, manner.

Traditionally, individuals earn through their efforts (individual at work), investments generate returns (money at work), and businesses leverage their workforce (people at work). It's essential to grasp this concept to understand the broader implications of organizational dynamics.

In viewing individuals as a work unit within an org chart, there's a need for a guiding principle—a guard rail. The default perspective often leads to a hierarchical approach, which can often possess an outdated or even inhumane view of the workforce. Here, we introduce the accountability chart, emphasizing mutual accountability among team members.

Unlike the traditional org chart, the accountability chart introduces the concept of mutual accountability. Exploring this paradigm, we realize that, as leaders, we are accountable for much more to our team members than they are to us. This makes business owners and leaders carry a heavy responsibility for tangible things and intangibles like safety and helping individuals grow. Though not easily articulated, this load plays a key role in the leadership journey. Hence, it's essential to acknowledge and explore this mutual accountability as a foundational aspect of the leadership process. This mutual accountability extends beyond mere job responsibilities to creating a conducive work environment, ensuring financial stability, and fostering personal growth for every team member.

"Getting People Done"

Building a culture of mutual accountability proves valuable. It is vital to shift the focus from getting work done through people to "getting people done" through the work we do. This amendment is central to cultivating a workplace where personal and professional growth are prioritized.

The term "getting people done" signifies our commitment to aiding individuals in becoming a greater version of themselves. Embracing the concept of "becoming," we recognize the continuous journey toward improvement. By actively contributing to the growth of our team members, we strive to help them move confidently toward a more significant future. This encapsulates our approach to getting people done through the work that we do.

Essentially, the shift from the traditional org chart to the accountability chart signifies an enhanced approach to organizational dynamics—one that values mutual accountability, prioritizes people's growth, and seeks to create a culture where individuals are not just seen as contributors but as partners in a shared journey of becoming.

Shifting Mindsets

This transition of moving away from an organizational chart mentality toward mutual accountability can be challenging, requiring introspection and honest evaluation. Here's a trick to make it easier: List five to ten things you are accountable to your colleagues or employees for. The items on this list could range from providing a safe work environment to being punctual and maintaining open communication.

Taking the time to document these accountabilities helps make the necessary shift from thinking as a leader with employees responsible for fulfilling your needs to being a teammate where all parties are responsible and accountable to one another. A mutually accountable mindset is the foundation for building a culture of accountability, emphasizing the reciprocal nature of responsibilities within a team.

Visualizing Value

One of the first steps toward fostering accountability is understanding the intrinsic value each person brings to the collective table. Despite occupying different roles, everyone is seated at the same table, contributing uniquely. The lens through which we perceive our colleagues and subordinates plays an essential role in shaping the work environment.

Consider the people around you and reflect on your interactions with them. You can perform this simple exercise: Identify three individuals you closely collaborate with daily. If you are in a leadership position, choose three employees working under you. Now ask yourself, "Do I see these individuals solely as a means to accomplish our goals, or do I recognize and appreciate their inherent value toward those goals?" If the answer is anything less than, "I appreciate the inherent and unique value they bring," it's time to visualize their value, identify their individual support toward the goals, and appreciate the contributions they bring.

Dan Sullivan, co-founder of Strategic Coach®, calls this a person's Unique Ability®. It isn't a static trait; rather, it's a dynamic, evolving aspect of oneself. It's the belief that each individual possesses inherent capabilities akin to factory-installed software in a computer's operating system.

There's an inherent uniqueness within each person, a set of innate abilities that make them distinct. This uniqueness, often overlooked, is like unwrapping a present, revealing layer after layer of capabilities. As we navigate life and gain a deeper understanding of ourselves, this Unique Ability becomes more apparent, evolving beyond just what we do to encompass who we are.

Maturity and Self-Discovery

Here, we can employ Shakespeare's timeless wisdom, "Know thyself and to thine own self be true," to understand that Unique Ability takes time. It essentially suggests maturity facilitates this process, with the belief that true self-discovery often comes with age and experience. As individuals mature, they unearth the layers of their unique abilities, becoming more authentic and comfortable in their skin.

Discovering Unique Abilities Through The ABC Model™

The ABC Model is represented by three circles, each capturing different aspects of daily activities. List every activity you engage in each day within these circles without assigning names yet.

Circle One: Irritating
Activities that are irksome and bothersome to you.

Circle Two: Okay
Activities that are neutral and don't particularly bother you.

Circle Three: Fascinating and Motivating
Activities that captivate and drive your enthusiasm.

In the past, personal irritations were assumed to be universal. However, understanding that what's irritating to one person might be fascinating to another is a transformative realization. This shift in perspective becomes integral to building a Unique Ability team.

Leader as a Conductor in the ABC Journey

The leader's role is akin to a conductor in a symphony, harmonizing the various unique abilities within the team. Each member contributes to different sections, such as the horn, string, and percussion sections. The conductor's skill lies in making these sections cohesive while recognizing that non-uniqueness in one area might be another's Unique Ability.

The beauty of a Unique Ability team emerges when diverse skills are brought together. Recognizing and valuing each team member's Unique Ability fosters a level of appreciation rarely seen in today's marketplace. It emphasizes that one person's non-uniqueness might be another's rare and valuable skill.

In summary, the ABC Model serves as a powerful tool for self-discovery, mutual accountability, and crafting a harmonious Unique Ability, thus encouraging a workplace culture that values and celebrates the diversity of individual strengths.

Saying "No" to Find Your Best "Yes"

Another primary aspect of accountability is learning to say "No." Saying "Yes" to everything can lead to a dilution of focus and effectiveness. Evaluate each opportunity in light of your unique abilities and determine whether saying "Yes" aligns with your goals.

The power of saying "No" lies in establishing and maintaining healthy boundaries, enabling you to prioritize your time, energy, and resources. This deliberate choice allows you to preserve energy and prevent burnout and exhaustion while respecting and valuing your time.

Moreover, it contributes to building self-confidence as you learn to make choices based on your needs rather than external pressures. Clearly and confidently communicating your boundaries fosters healthy relationships by preventing over-commitment, ultimately leading to a more balanced and fulfilling life.

Saying "No" isn't about rejecting opportunities negatively; it's a strategic and mindful way to prioritize your best "Yes," aligning with your unique abilities and long-term objectives.

How Jesus Demonstrated Accountability

Let's look at how Jesus can inspire us regarding accountability. Jesus showed a deep sense of responsibility in his actions. He was strongly committed to a higher purpose — a divine mission centered on love, redemption, and compassion.

In his service to others, Jesus consistently demonstrated accountability. Whether he was healing the sick, feeding the hungry, or comforting the distressed, he took responsibility for the well-being of those he served. In the famous Good Samaritan story, Jesus highlighted the importance of being accountable to our neighbors, no matter our differences. His teachings stressed the interconnectedness of humanity, emphasizing the need for mutual accountability in creating a compassionate and fair community.

The Ultimate Act of Accountability

The highest demonstration of Jesus' accountability was his crucifixion. Despite facing immense suffering, he steadily committed to a divine purpose and felt accountable for humanity's salvation. This selfless act is a powerful example of accountability, showing how an individual's actions can profoundly impact others for the greater good.

Embracing Jesus as a model of accountability offers inspiration in his actions and how he handled complex relationships. He consistently prioritized love, justice, and the well-being of those around him. As we aim for accountability in our lives, Jesus' example can guide us, reminding us that true accountability goes beyond personal interests and is rooted in a higher purpose of service and love.

Simplifying Complexity

Implementing these strategies to attain accountability might seem like a substantial effort, especially when working with others. While the process can be demanding, the potential rewards make it worthwhile. However, I understand that it might sound overwhelming, almost like orchestrating chaos, particularly when assembling diverse individuals with distinct strengths and emphasizing enhancing those strengths rather than focusing on weaknesses.

In contemplating this, I'm reminded of the metaphorical concept of the ceiling of complexity in our life's journey, regardless of our definition of success, which extends beyond financial achievements. Life transitions, such as moving from being single to entering a relationship and then into marriage, introduce complexity. This complexity, while chosen and positive, increases as we add elements like having children intentionally. Success in life accumulates complexities and, at times, chaos. The ceiling of complexity emerges when our lives become so complicated that further progress seems hindered unless we find a breakthrough. This is where something needs to change, and breaking through this ceiling requires embracing a fundamental principle: simplicity.

Simplicity becomes the key to breaking through the ceiling of complexity. It's not just a simple word but a challenging action. The simplification process lies in recognizing and addressing what's irritating, okay, fascinating, or motivating in our lives. Utilizing the ABC model, especially when facing a complexity ceiling, helps identify areas that need simplification. The principle involves eliminating irritating elements, delegating tasks, and amplifying activities that are fascinating or motivating. Consider the example of a bothersome task, like mowing the lawn, which could be outsourced to someone else, like a neighborhood kid or even your significant other, if it aligns with their unique abilities. In simplifying, it's about making decisions to eliminate what adds unnecessary complexity and increasing focus on what truly matters.

Accountability is not a burdensome imposition but a liberating force. It empowers individuals to live their best lives by recognizing their unique abilities, fostering mutual accountability within teams, and simplifying complexities. The journey toward accountability is transformative, unlocking new levels of capability and opportunity.

As you explore this path, remember the wise words of Warren Buffet. "The difference between successful people and very successful people is very successful people say no to almost everything." Embrace simplicity, say no to the unnecessary, and watch as the ceiling of complexity shatters, giving way to a clearer and more productive path forward.

Let your conversation be always full of grace, seasoned with salt, so you may know how to answer everyone.
—Colossians 4:5-6

CHAPTER SEVEN

COMMUNICATION

Communication

My dear brothers and sisters, take note of this: Everyone should be quick to listen, slow to speak and slow to become angry.
—James 1:19

Communication is the process of exchanging information, ideas, thoughts, and feelings between individuals or groups through appropriate channels and mediums. It involves encoding messages by the sender and deciphering them by the receiver, intending to convey the intended meaning.

The above bible verse highlights essential principles for effective communication: attentive listening, measured speech, and emotional regulation. When we speak thoughtfully and deliberately, we convey messages clearly and respectfully, nurturing understanding and trust. Moreover, the counsel to remain calm in the face of provocation promotes emotional maturity, fostering constructive dialogue and conflict resolution. These principles advocate a communication style grounded in patience, empathy, and self-discipline.

Communication as a Key Guardrail

Communication stands as a vital guardrail in protecting our hearts. It goes beyond the words we speak, encompassing body language, facial expressions, and actions. For instance, punctuality communicates respect for others' time and demonstrates value. Moreover, communication isn't just about the medium—whether it's texting, DMing, or TikToking. Instead, it's about the deeper value and impact of what we convey and how it affects others.

Over-communicating vs. Under-communicating

We often say, "Little harm comes from over-communicating, but under-communicating leads to problems." Under-communicating can lead to a multitude of disadvantages within various contexts, whether it be in personal relationships, professional settings, or team collaborations. Reflecting on our individual experiences, we've all likely encountered situations where inadequate communication caused issues. Whether it's a missed deadline due to unclear instructions, a misunderstanding with a loved one because feelings were not expressed openly, or a project setback because team members failed to communicate effectively, the negative consequences of under-communication are all too familiar.

Not only that, but less communication fosters misunderstandings, ambiguity, and uncertainty, which can result in conflicts, inefficiencies, and missed opportunities. Lack of clear communication inhibits the sharing of ideas, goals, and expectations, hindering progress and growth. Besides, under-communicating can erode trust and morale, as individuals may feel excluded, undervalued, or uninformed, ultimately impeding cooperation and cohesion. The drawbacks of under-communicating underscore the importance of open, transparent, and frequent communication for promoting understanding, alignment, and success in any endeavor.

Hence, when it comes to words, it's better to over-communicate than under-communicate. By ensuring clarity and transparency in our communication, we demonstrate respect and consideration for others.

In essence, communication isn't just about what we say—it's about how we say it and what our actions convey. Effective communication ensures that everyone understands their roles, responsibilities, and objectives clearly. Effective communication helps to avoid misunderstandings and confusion, leading to better productivity and efficiency in the workplace. Additionally, employees are more likely to be engaged and motivated when they feel informed and involved.

The 10-Minute Rule

The "10-Minute Rule," a practice within our team, defines a principle emphasizing timely and responsive interaction.

For instance, if a team member receives a message or a call, they are expected to respond within 10 minutes. This rule serves as more than just a guideline; it's a mutual agreement among team members to over-communicate when necessary. It underscores the significance we place on any form of communication—be it a call or a message—as a signal for immediate attention or assistance. Embracing this practice showcases our commitment to respecting each other's time and needs.

For example, during project meetings, adhering to the 10-Minute Rule means promptly addressing any questions or concerns raised by colleagues, preventing delays in decision-making and project progress. Similarly, in urgent situations requiring immediate assistance, such as technical issues or client inquiries, team members prioritize swift responses within the designated timeframe, ensuring efficient problem resolution and client satisfaction.

By adhering to this proactive approach, we facilitate smoother workflows and foster a collective sense of purpose and support. It reinforces the idea that we are all essential components of a unified team striving towards shared success.

The Power of Actions in Communication

I've always believed in leading by example, where actions speak louder than words. Instead of "practice what I preach," it's about "preaching what I practice." It's an assurance that I not only talk the talk, but I walk it too. This distinction is essential because our actions are able to reinforce and authenticate the message being conveyed. While words provide the foundation of communication, actions serve as a tangible demonstration of commitment, sincerity, and intent. Actions lend credibility to words, making them more convincing and impactful. Whether following through on promises, embodying values through behavior, or expressing emotions through gestures, actions provide clarity and depth to communication, ensuring that the intended message is heard, understood, and believed.

Fundamentally, actions serve as the bridge between words and results, facilitating genuine connection, trust, and effectiveness in communication. Our small actions, such as showing up on time and being dressed appropriately, send a powerful message of respect and commitment. It's a sad reality that simply showing up can set us apart, but it emphasizes the importance of consistency and reliability in communication.

The Laws of Attraction: Becoming a Magnet

"You are a living magnet." This quote from Brian Tracy's book, "Maximum Achievement," encapsulates the idea that our thoughts and mindset have a powerful influence on what we attract into our lives. It suggests we are like magnets, drawing in people and circumstances that resonate with our dominant thoughts and beliefs.

Jim Rohn's statement, "You're the average of the five people you spend the most time with," complements this concept by bringing our attention to the significant impact of our social circle on our personal development. He proposes that we become a reflection of the five individuals we spend the most time with. This implies that the attitudes, values, and behaviors of those closest to us shape our outlook and character.

Known as the Dean of Personal Development, Earl Nightingale echoes a similar sentiment. "We become what we think about most of the time." This reinforces how we mirror the characteristics of those around us. He highlights the tendency for individuals to adopt the traits and habits of those they surround themselves with, indicating the importance of choosing our companions wisely. Furthermore, King Solomon's timeless advice urges us to guard our hearts, for it plays an indispensable role in shaping our lives.

Though expressed in different ways, these teachings converge on a singular truth: our environment significantly impacts our trajectory. Whether we're soaring like eagles or scratching with turkeys, our surroundings shape our journey, magnifying the importance of cultivating a conducive environment where healthy communication thrives.

Here, we must understand that effective communication isn't about eloquence or formal education; it's about how our actions speak volumes and how we show respect to others through our interactions. By prioritizing respectful and mindful communication in our lives, we naturally attract others who share our values. Our actions in prioritizing communication serve as a beacon, drawing in individuals who appreciate and reciprocate this respect.

The Platinum Rule: Honoring Individual Differences

In our exploration of effective communication strategies, a familiar rule emerges—the Golden Rule: "Do unto others as you would have them do unto you," which advises treating others as we would like to be treated. This principle reiterates the significance of showing respect and appreciation for others, encouraging harmonious relationships through positive interactions. Yet, as we dive deeper into the convolutions of communication dynamics, we uncover a more refined principle—the Platinum Rule.

The Platinum Rule, articulated in the book "People Smart," by Melvin L. Silberman and Freda Hansburg, introduces a nuanced perspective beyond mere reciprocity. While the Golden Rule accentuates empathy and consideration, the Platinum Rule elevates this concept by urging us to recognize and honor individual differences—acknowledging that each person possesses unique preferences, perspectives, and communication styles.

Unlike the Golden Rule, which assumes that others desire the same treatment we desire, the Platinum Rule encourages us to tailor our interactions to the preferences of others. It prompts us to consider not only how we wish to be treated but also how others prefer to be treated. By embracing this principle, we appreciate diversity and honor the unique attributes of each individual.

Embracing Complexity

Essentially, the Platinum Rule is akin to realizing that a coin has not just two but three sides—heads, tails, and the edge. In today's polarized environment, where differing opinions often lead to division, embracing this edge becomes paramount. Standing on the edge of the coin symbolizes wisdom, where one examines both sides of the equation. This level of discernment is a hallmark of true intelligence, something that we seem to have lost sight of in many aspects of life.

In the past, structured debates taught us the importance of taking a stance while respecting opposing views. However, these principles seem to have faded in modern discourse. Yet, honoring the diversity of perspectives is integral to effective communication. In this way, recognizing and embracing both sides of the equation allows us to respect the complexity of human interaction and pave the way for meaningful dialogue.

The Platinum Rule challenges us to go beyond surface-level interactions, understanding and respecting the unique needs and perspectives of others. As we stand on the edge of the coin, we acknowledge the richness of diversity and strive for genuine connection and understanding in our communication.

Choosing Your Path: The Power of Discipline and Attitude

In our journey of understanding communication, it's vital to acknowledge that it's a discipline—a practice that requires commitment and effort. Just as discipline shapes our actions and attitudes, so does the discipline of communication. We're presented with a choice: to follow the path of intentional communication or to disregard its significance. The direction we choose ultimately shapes the quality of our connections and experiences.

Finally, it's our attitude that influences not only the tone and dynamics of communication but also its outcomes. As Charles Swindoll famously said, "Attitude is more important than facts. It is more important than the past, than education, money, circumstances, than failures and success, than what other people think, say, or do. It is more important than appearance, ability, or skill. It will make or break a business, a home, a friendship, an organization."

We all possess the power to choose our attitude, just as we choose our approach to communication. By investing time and energy into meaningful communication with the right attitude and mindset, we enrich our relationships and achieve success in collaborative endeavors.

The Payoff: Rich Relationships

At the heart of intentional communication lies the promise of rich, fulfilling relationships. Whether in marriage, family, or professional settings, effective communication is the cornerstone of healthy connections. As we find our way through this worldly dynamic, prioritizing communication ensures that we nurture and sustain the relationships that matter most.

Remember, communication is not merely a tool but a guiding principle that shapes our life experiences. When we abide by the discipline of communication, we pave the way for deeper connections, mutual understanding, and a more rewarding life journey.

How Jesus Illustrated the Significance of Communication

Throughout the New Testament, Jesus exemplifies the profound importance of communication through his teachings, parables, and interactions with others. His words and actions offer timeless lessons on effective communication, compassion, and understanding.

First and foremost, Jesus' approach to communication was multi-faceted. He frequently demonstrated compassionate listening, showing empathy and understanding towards those he encountered. In the Gospel of Matthew (Matthew 9:36), it is written: "When he saw the crowds, he had compassion for them, because they were harassed and helpless, like sheep without a shepherd."

In his teachings and parables, Jesus used clear and relatable language to convey philosophical truths. In Matthew 13:34-35, it is stated: "Jesus spoke all these things to the crowd in parables; he did not say anything to them without using a parable. So was fulfilled what was spoken through the prophet: 'I will open my mouth in parables; I will utter things hidden since the creation of the world.'" Jesus' use of parables allowed him to communicate complex spiritual concepts in a way that resonated with his audience.

It's worth noting that Jesus engaged in respectful dialogue with individuals from all walks of life, regardless of their social status or background. In John 4:7-26, Jesus has an insightful conversation with a Samaritan woman at the well, treating her with dignity and respect despite societal norms.

Above all, Jesus emphasized the importance of speaking truth with love and grace. The Epistle to the Ephesians (Ephesians 4:15) is written, "Instead, speaking the truth in love, we will grow to become in every respect the mature body of him who is the head, that is, Christ." This verse is enough for us to understand the value of honest and compassionate communication in promoting spiritual growth and unity within the community of believers.

In summary, Jesus' approach to communication involved addressing felt needs, building relationships, and engaging with people in their cultural context. He effectively employed principles such as active listening, guided speaking, multisensory engagement, and gentle responding to meet the needs of diverse audiences. Hence, Jesus' teachings exemplify timeless principles of effective communication and relationship-building. His holistic approach, rooted in empathy, authenticity, and cultural sensitivity, is a compelling model for individuals seeking to nurture meaningful bonds and engage with others in a transformative way.

For we aim at what is honorable not only in the Lord's sight but also in the sight of man.
—2 Corinthians 8:21

CHAPTER EIGHT

INTEGRITY

Integrity

The integrity of the upright guides them, but the unfaithful are destroyed by their duplicity.
—Proverbs 11:3

The first part of the biblical verse emphasizes that individuals who possess integrity, who are honest, principled, and morally upright, are guided by these qualities. Integrity acts as a moral compass, directing their actions and decisions.

Conversely, those who lack integrity, who are deceitful, dishonest, or two-faced (duplicity means deceitfulness or double-dealing), will ultimately face negative consequences.

Their lack of honesty and trustworthiness can lead to their downfall or destruction.

Redefining Integrity: Beyond the Clichés

Integrity is a term often thrown around in organizational mission statements, but what does it truly mean?

During the development of GRACIE, our team grappled with defining integrity. It transcended mere adherence to promises and encompassed a broader spectrum of values and ethical considerations. This evolution prompted us to rethink integrity as a foundational aspect of our guardrails—guiding principles aimed at safeguarding our hearts and actions.

While integrity is commonly associated with honesty and ethics, its essence extends beyond surface-level definitions. Integrity manifests in our actions, shaping how we conduct ourselves in various contexts. Whether it's honoring commitments, practicing transparency, or upholding ethical standards, integrity is a guiding force in our interactions and behaviors.

I was a financial advisor in the mid-2000s. During the annual firm element test, which all securities professionals in America are required to take, I encountered a thought-provoking question: "Ethics is always changing: true or false?" I confidently answered false, believing that ethical principles remain constant over time. However, to my surprise, my answer was deemed incorrect. It was a moment of realization for me, as it highlighted a fundamental disagreement between my perspective and the prevailing view among those who designed the test. While I firmly believe in the existence of ethical absolutes, the test suggested that ethics is a dynamic and evolving concept. This discrepancy became a significant turning point for me, akin to the final straw that broke the camel's back. It prompted me to reevaluate my career path, leading me to ultimately decide to leave the financial industry after twenty-five years as a Wall Street insider.

Reclaiming True North: The Role of Integrity

I've had firsthand experience working in the financial services industry, and I can assert that Wall Street operates within an inherently skewed system. While it may sound blunt, it's a reality I've observed over the years. I don't intend to delve into conspiracy theories; rather, I base this assertion on historical facts. The securities laws we abide by today were established in response to widespread fraud in the 1920s, culminating in the stock market crash of 1929 and subsequent depression. These laws were put in place to protect Main Street investors from being exploited.

Despite these regulations, the game has evolved, becoming even more rigged, particularly with advancements in technology, microchip usage, and algorithmic trading. In the past, news was disseminated through newspapers or radio broadcasts, with updates arriving intermittently. Now, with information available instantly at our fingertips, trading occurs at lightning speed. This rapid pace, coupled with insider information and automated trading, further tilts the playing field in favor of those with the means to exploit it.

This systemic bias makes it increasingly challenging for average investors to achieve long-term financial success. The traditional advice of "buy, hold, and diversify" is losing its effectiveness in the face of these evolving dynamics. When Wall Street suggests that ethics are constantly evolving, it implies flexibility in the rules, which further reinforces the notion of a rigged system.

So, when discussing integrity, it's essential to consider whether there's a true north—a set of unwavering principles guiding one's actions. Integrity isn't just about personal conduct; it's about upholding principles within oneself, within organizations, and in relationships. It's about maintaining a moral compass despite the shifting landscape of the financial world.

Integrity: A Matter of Internal Alignment

Ultimately, cultivating integrity involves mastering self-leadership—a profound ability to guide oneself with honesty and conviction. Before we can effectively lead others, we must learn to lead ourselves well. This involves being accountable for our actions, making choices that align with our values, and actively shaping our environment to support our growth.

Integrity, often regarded as a cornerstone of character, finds its roots in internal alignment rather than external circumstances. It goes beyond our actions or appearances, delving into the realm of self-leadership and personal development. True integrity emanates from within, shaping how individuals navigate their lives and relationships.

History abounds with examples of individuals thrust into leadership roles yet lacking in self-mastery. Such instances serve as cautionary tales, highlighting the inherent link between personal integrity and effective leadership.

Biblical teachings further emphasize the significance of internal governance. The adage "If you can't manage your own household well, how can you manage God's affairs?" underlines the importance of self-leadership in matters of integrity. This principle aptly explains the importance of tending to one's internal affairs as a precursor to assuming external responsibilities.

Honesty with oneself is paramount. Despite our self-perceptions, there are invariably areas where growth is needed. Drawing from timeless wisdom, the principle "faithful in little, faithful in much" underscores the significance of integrity in both minor and major tasks.

Moreover, self-reflection can be challenging. Here, seeking external perspectives can offer valuable insights into our relationships and help us gain clarity on areas where we might feel stuck.

Starting Small: The Foundation of Integrity

Integrity shows up in the little things we do every day, even in situations that might seem unimportant. Let's say you had a small accident with your car recently. You could have easily ignored the damage, but you chose to be honest about it. This shows that integrity isn't just about big actions; it's part of our everyday life.

Integrity starts with being faithful to even the smallest tasks and duties. Whether it's a major repair or a tiny obligation, the principle remains the same. Every choice we make, no matter how small, adds to our integrity.

To sum up, building integrity means being honest, reflecting on our actions, and staying true to our responsibilities, no matter how insignificant they might seem. By focusing on integrity in the small things, we set a foundation for behaving ethically and growing personally.

Importance of Surroundings

When considering personal growth, one significant aspect to discuss is the influence of our surroundings and environment. We've often heard the adage that we are the sum of the five people we spend the most time with, highlighting the profound impact our environment can have on us. Therefore, it's crucial to be mindful of our environment and to actively protect it.

Recently, I've been mentoring a young man who is becoming increasingly aware of the positive changes in his life. He's breaking free from past struggles and detrimental habits, steering towards a new path. However, this journey often requires him to distance himself from toxic environments, which can be challenging, especially when those environments involve people.

Choosing Relationships Wisely

As the saying goes, the individuals who helped us out of difficult times may not necessarily be the ones to guide us toward our goals. While we cannot choose our family relationships, we do have the choice of selecting other relationships in our lives.

Additionally, when it comes to choosing the people we surround ourselves with, it's vital to take a moment to reflect on our internal state and how it manifests in our external world. This process of introspection, as mentioned previously, sheds light on the dynamics of our relationships and the stories they tell.

Choosing relationships wisely is a multifaceted process that involves self-reflection, seeking external perspectives, and implementing practical steps for growth. By understanding the connection between our internal state and external reality, we can form relationships with greater clarity and integrity.

Identifying Patterns

Reflecting on patterns in our lives is essential for growth. Patterns can manifest in various aspects of our lives, such as relationships, career choices, or even our emotional responses to certain situations. Whether it's a pattern of repeated divorces, frequent job changes, or constantly shifting relationships, there is often a common thread that connects these occurrences. Recognizing these patterns requires a level of self-reflection and honesty that can be challenging but is essential for personal development.

For instance, if someone finds themselves repeatedly experiencing failed relationships, they need to examine common themes or behaviors that may contribute to this pattern. They might discover patterns of communication issues, a tendency to avoid vulnerability, or a fear of commitment. Similarly, someone who constantly changes jobs might need to explore underlying reasons such as dissatisfaction with their career path, difficulty in maintaining focus, or a fear of failure.

Confronting these patterns requires a willingness to be brutally honest with oneself. It involves acknowledging and accepting personal shortcomings, insecurities, and past mistakes. This process can be uncomfortable and even painful at times, but it is necessary for growth. Without honest self-assessment, individuals may continue to repeat the same patterns and find themselves stuck in cycles of frustration and dissatisfaction.

Once patterns are identified, the next step is understanding the role we play in perpetuating them. This requires taking responsibility for our actions and choices. Rather than blaming external circumstances or other people, we must recognize the impact of our decisions on our lives. This level of accountability empowers us to make positive changes and break free from destructive patterns.

How Jesus Exemplified Integrity in His Life

Jesus exemplified integrity in various aspects of his life, teachings, and actions, as recorded in the New Testament. One notable demonstration of his integrity is his unwavering commitment to truthfulness and honesty. In John 14:6, Jesus declares, "I am the way, the truth, and the life." This statement reflects his steadfast adherence to truth as a fundamental principle. Throughout his ministry, Jesus consistently spoke the truth, even when it was unpopular or inconvenient. He rebuked hypocrisy and challenged the prevailing norms of his time, emphasizing the importance of sincerity and authenticity.

Furthermore, Jesus illustrated integrity through his actions, which aligned with his words. In Matthew 5:37, he instructs his followers to let their "Yes" be yes and their "No" be no, indicating the importance of integrity in keeping promises and fulfilling commitments. Jesus lived out this principle impeccably, consistently fulfilling his divine mission and remaining faithful to his Father's will, even in the face of adversity and temptation. His actions were always congruent with his teachings, demonstrating a harmonious integration of belief and behavior.

Besides, Jesus' integrity is evident in his obedience to God's will, even in the face of personal sacrifice and suffering. In the Garden of Gethsemane, Jesus prays, "Father, if you are willing, take this cup from me; yet not my will, but yours be done" (Luke 22:42). Despite the agony he faced, Jesus submits himself entirely to the Father's plan, demonstrating his unyielding integrity and devotion to fulfilling his Divine purpose. His willingness to endure persecution, humiliation, and, ultimately, death on the cross epitomizes the depth of his integrity and commitment to righteousness and is a prime example of self-leadership.

Otherwise, you may say in your heart, "My power and the strength of my hand made me this wealth."
—Deuteronomy 8:17

CHAPTER NINE

ENERGY

Energy

> *My flesh and my heart may fail, but God is the strength of my heart and my portion forever.*
> —Psalm 73:26

The first part of the above verse acknowledges the physical and emotional limitations of human existence. It implies that our bodies and hearts are susceptible to weariness, illness, and ultimately mortality. Essentially, this could refer to the finite nature of our physical and emotional energy reserves. We have only so much capacity to endure physical challenges and emotional burdens. However, the next verse suggests that despite our limitations, there is a transcendent source of energy beyond ourselves, which could be understood as tapping into a spiritual or divine energy source. It's the recognition that when our energy falters, there is a higher power that can sustain us emotionally and provide the strength needed to persevere. Moreover, it suggests that this divine energy is not temporary but enduring, thus implying an infinite reservoir of strength one can draw upon, contrasting with the finite nature of human energy. Hence, the above verse speaks to finding sustenance and renewal in something beyond ourselves.

Energy and People

Energy is a vital component that permeates everything we do. Whether it's the electricity powering the lights above us or the adrenaline rush from witnessing fighter jets or fireworks, energy surrounds us constantly.

One aspect of energy that often goes unnoticed is its connection to the people around us. The individuals we interact with carry their unique energies, which can greatly influence our demeanor and motivation. For instance, though unseen by the audience, the crew working behind the scenes of a Broadway show exudes an infectious energy that energizes everyone present.

Types of People Based on Energy

In discussing the dynamics of energy, it's evident that people can be categorized into two groups: "Batteries Included" (BIs) and "Batteries Not Included" (BNIs). The former refers to individuals who radiate positivity, enthusiasm, and drive—akin to having a battery that powers them. On the other hand, the latter lacks this inherent energy and may rely on external sources for motivation.

Being surrounded by "Batteries Included" individuals is desirable. Whether in professional settings like recruiting agents for financial services or in personal relationships, the presence of energetic and motivated individuals can significantly impact one's success and well-being.

Nonetheless, I've come to realize that, as gifted as I might be in motivation and energy, I'm not always capable of motivating others. It's important to acknowledge that I must surround myself with motivated individuals to thrive personally and professionally.

I've learned that having motivated individuals in my circle is crucial. Just like the concept of "batteries included," if someone lacks intrinsic motivation, it's challenging for me to energize them. Hence, I've recognized the necessity of hiring and associating with motivated individuals to foster a dynamic and productive environment.

Understanding Relationship Dynamics: Energizers vs. Stabilizers

My wife and I, who have been married for a long time, prioritize continuous learning and growth. Instead of waiting for issues to arise, we proactively seek opportunities for improvement. Attending a marriage conference recently reaffirmed our commitment to personal development and mutual enhancement within our relationship.

At the conference, we encountered an intriguing concept: the distinction between "energizers" and "stabilizers" within relationships. One partner typically leans more toward energizing, while the other tends to stabilize. This understanding provided us with a new perspective on our dynamic.

We understood that both roles are equally valuable in maintaining a balanced and fulfilling relationship. Whether one is predominantly an energizer or a stabilizer, each contributes uniquely to the partnership's harmony and growth.

However, having a harmonic balance doesn't mean our relationship is free of conflicts and arguments. Often, tensions arise when our natural tendencies clash, particularly when stepping outside our usual routines. Yet, we have intentionally established such an understanding that has enabled us to navigate conflicts more effectively and appreciate each other's strengths.

Ultimately, we've come to appreciate the importance of surrounding ourselves with individuals who share our drive for growth and progress. By fostering an environment conducive to learning and personal development, we enhance our relationships and individual journeys toward self-improvement. This commitment also allowed us to make simple yet meaningful changes in our varied approaches over time, resulting in profound transformations in our relationships and overall outlook on life.

Future-Oriented Thinking: The R-Factor Question®

In our discussions on energy and motivation, one concept that frequently arises is the distinction between past-based and future-based thinking. We often ponder, "What drives individuals to excel and progress personally and professionally?" One way to gauge this is what is called The R-Factor Question or the Relationship Question.

Imagine this scenario: three years from today, you and your friend are sitting down for a conversation, reflecting on the past three years of your lives. Your friend asks, "What would have had to happen during this time frame for you to be satisfied with your progress, both personally and professionally?"

Now, engaging with this R-Factor Question requires a forward-looking mindset. This consideration shifts the focus from dwelling on past achievements or failures to envisioning and planning for a brighter future. By contemplating what needs to occur for contentment and fulfillment three years down the line, you will ultimately demonstrate your capacity for future-based thinking. Therefore, if you can articulate clear objectives and aspirations for your future selves, you exhibit traits of future-based thinking.

Conversely, individuals entrenched in past-based thinking tend to reminisce excessively about past glories or setbacks, often clinging to outdated identities or achievements, such as recalling athletic triumphs from high school days. Looking back this way often hinders their ability to foster a proactive approach to life's challenges and opportunities. While reflecting on past experiences, whether from high school or college, can evoke a sense of nostalgia and fond memories, as we navigate through life, it's crucial to recognize that our best moments aren't confined to the past. Instead, they serve as valuable stepping stones toward a brighter future.

Hence, it's essential to realize the importance of future-based thinking by embracing the R-Factor Question as a tool for personal and professional growth. By shifting the focus toward envisioning and actively working toward desired futures, individuals can cultivate a mindset conducive to sustained progress and fulfillment.

The Role of Future-Based Thinking in Driving Energy

In cultivating dynamic and energized environments, we prioritize surrounding ourselves with individuals who embody a future-based perspective. Through their ability to envision and strive toward ambitious goals, these individuals infuse our organizations and communities with vitality and drive. Future-based thinking catalyzes innovation, growth, and continued motivation.

Reflecting on personal experiences, such as my entrepreneurial venture in my mid-20s, underscores the importance of embracing a future-oriented mindset. Despite encountering failure, the journey instilled valuable lessons and insights, highlighting the resilience and adaptability of future-based thinking.

The Seven Levels Deep Technique

There's a fascinating concept that's emerged known as "seven levels deep." This technique involves peeling back layers of motivation and understanding, similar to peeling back layers of an onion, where each layer represents a deeper level of understanding and introspection.

At its core, the "seven levels deep" approach acknowledges that surface-level motivations, such as desires for financial security or material success, often only scratch the surface of what truly drives an individual. By systematically delving deeper into one's motivations, individuals can gain a more comprehensive understanding of their values, fears, and aspirations.

The process involves asking a series of questions, each probing deeper into the underlying reasons behind a particular goal or desire. For example, someone may initially express a desire for financial security. However, by asking "Why is financial security important to you?" multiple times, participants are encouraged to explore the deeper layers of their motivations. This deeper understanding, in turn, enables them to form a more nuanced and authentic vision for their future. As they deeply understand the core of their desires, they unlock new avenues for personal growth and fulfillment.

Integrating Integrity and Energy

While seemingly distinct, integrity and energy are intricately linked, often fusing our actions and decisions. Self-leadership and energy are closely intertwined facets of personal effectiveness, shaping our ability to navigate challenges and pursue our goals.

Integrity encompasses adherence to moral and ethical principles, guiding our conduct and decisions. On the other hand, energy pertains to the vitality and enthusiasm we bring to our endeavors. While complementary, each plays a discrete role in determining our outcomes.

The Power of Goal Setting

As individuals, we face a fundamental question each morning: Are we "batteries included" or "not included" people?

This distinction is not merely a matter of disposition but a discipline and decision that nurtures our outlook and interactions with others. See, external sources cannot instill energy within us; rather, it must emanate from within.

Positive energy is a courageous and contagious force that propels us forward, infusing our actions and interactions with vitality and purpose. However, there are instances where we find ourselves lacking in energy, often due to a lack of clarity regarding our future goals.

Here, a staggering reality confronts us: most individuals lack concrete goals for their future. Less than 20 percent of men and women have their goals documented vividly, and even fewer regularly review them.[3] While many acknowledge the importance of setting goals, far fewer take the necessary steps to actualize them.

Goals guide us toward a future that we envision for ourselves. By committing to become goal-setting, goal-achieving individuals, we gain a sense of agency and control over our destinies. Future-based thinking becomes a hallmark of our approach to life, allowing us to tackle the challenges with clarity and purpose.

---

[3] Murphy, M. (2018, April 15). *Neuroscience Explains Why You Need To Write Down Your Goals If You Actually Want To Achieve Them.* Forbes. https://www.forbes.com/sites/markmurphy/2018/04/15/neuroscience-explains-why-you-need-to-write-down-your-goals-if-you-actually-want-to-achieve-them/?sh=51379c437905

How Jesus Demonstrated Energy in His Life

Jesus demonstrated energy through his tireless dedication to his mission and ability to inspire and empower others. Throughout the New Testament, we see Jesus tirelessly traveling from place to place, teaching, healing, and spreading his message of love and salvation. In Mark 6:31, it's mentioned, "Then, because so many people were coming and going that they did not even have a chance to eat, he said to them, 'Come with me by yourselves to a quiet place and get some rest.'" Even though Jesus recognized the need for rest, his commitment to his mission often led him to forgo personal comfort to minister to others, displaying his boundless energy and unwavering dedication to his purpose.

Moreover, Jesus' energy was evident in his actions and ability to impart strength and vitality to those around him. In Matthew 11:28-30, Jesus says, "Come to me, all you who are weary and burdened, and I will give you rest. Take my yoke upon you and learn from me, for I am gentle and humble in heart, and you will find rest for your souls. For my yoke is easy, and my burden is light." Here, Jesus offers solace and rejuvenation to those who are tired and burdened, demonstrating his ability to provide spiritual energy and renewal. His words and presence infused hope and empowerment into the lives of countless individuals, showcasing the transformative power of his energy and compassion. The energy Jesus offers touches the deepest levels of our souls and impacts everything in our lives. The rest follows suit when our hearts move from the root energy of what Jesus has done and is doing in our souls. Our mental, physical, financial, and emotional aspects of who we are are fed and given energy. It's pretty impressive!

Simplifying the Takeaway

Embracing positive energy and meaningful goals is crucial for deciding the trajectory of both our personal and professional lives. Through introspection, goal setting, and impactful interactions, we pave the way for a brighter, more fulfilling journey of self-discovery and growth. Let us stay dedicated to leaving a positive legacy and making a lasting impact. I urge you to reflect on your journey of growth and self-improvement, developing a mindset of lifelong learning and envisioning a future beyond your past. Seize the opportunity to assess yourself, explore your potential, and continue advancing toward personal and professional fulfillment.

*You, my brothers and sisters, were called to be free.
But do not use your freedom to indulge the flesh; rather,
serve one another humbly in love.*
—Galatians 5:13

CHAPTER TEN

CLOSING

GRACIE, what an amazing concept! She's irreplaceable in my life and Jeff's. Jeff opened this intro book to GRACIE, and I will finish it before we jump into the next full book about gratitude.

Developing GRACIE from a concept that floated in our heads and our hearts and publishing it as a book has been extraordinary. The soul searching has been challenging and time-consuming, but overall, the process has been encouraging and clarifying. The lens of GRACIE is different than what most see the world through. The different tint of GRACIE's glasses opens up our views to new colors, dreams, and realizations.

I want to encourage you and let you know that you may be surprised by what you see and how you see things when you begin embracing GRACIE. My guess is that, more often than not, you'll be more surprised as you realize how others around you see life. Choosing to read this intro to GRACIE and the next six books, one for each letter of GRACIE will put you on a different playing field than others. What you learn through these books will teach you to value your experiences in a different way and stretch your current paradigm.

I loved it when we talked earlier in this book about being the sum of the five people closest to you. What a profound reality! At this time in my life, I have a beautiful wife and three gorgeous girls aged six, nine, and thirteen. Their worlds are full of wonder and excitement. New things happen daily, and new skills and worlds are created in their minds and imaginations. It's extremely refreshing for me to slow down and be part of that. Moving from my world of complexity, hurry, ups and downs of business, and decision-making to theirs is like water in the desert. It puts me in a state of gratitude very quickly.

I've vacationed in numerous different places with my wife and girls. We enjoy seeing new things and activities—from RV trips to sitting on a beach to hiking in the mountains. There are a few memories that illustrate my point above. On a number of these trips, we inevitably have a house near or on a golf course. I'm not a huge golfer, but I'll have fun and enjoy the company. It's not like we picked the house for the golf course.

Usually, on these trips, we'll be at the house when the golf course sprinklers go on randomly. If you've ever seen golf course sprinklers, they are big and powerful. It's truly impressive how much water they shoot out over such a huge distance. I started something when my oldest was young, probably five or six. Because you never know how long the sprinklers stay on, if we saw them running, I would ask, "Do you want to run in the sprinkler right now?" If they said "Yes," a fury of crazy would follow as we sprinted out in our clothes or quickly changed into swimming suits and rushed to run through before they shut off. It's exciting, crazy, and takes me to a world of simple wonder. We were filled with child-like wonder for a short period, affirming we could live in the moment, stand under a sprinkler, and let a simple but incredibly memorable ritual refresh our souls.

As you finish this book and read the books to come, I encourage you to embrace GRACIE and let your soul be refreshed. It needs it; you need it; your family and loved ones need it. Lead the way in this refreshment with those around you by embracing GRACIE and allowing her to protect your heart, your life source.

But whoever looks intently into the perfect law that gives freedom and continues in it—not forgetting what they have heard, but doing it—they will be blessed in what they do.
—James 1:25

RECOMMENDED READING AND OTHER RESOURCES

Other Books from the Authors:

Purpose, Passion & Profit — This powerful book includes transformational stories from Jeff Huston and other unstoppable super achievers about how purpose, passion, and profit set them on the path to success. These stories seek to create positive, everlasting change in your life and move you toward action!

The Little Church (Big God Books) — Big God Books help children see how God works through everyday miracles and are a resource for parents to speak quickly and straightforwardly about the power of our Big God.

The Gap and The Gain® **by Dan Sullivan with Dr. Benjamin Hardy** — In this book, you will learn that measuring your current self vs. your former self has enormous psychological benefits. That's really the key to this deceptively simple yet multi-layered concept that will have you feeling good, feeling grateful, and feeling like you are making progress even when times are tough, which will, in turn, bolster motivation, confidence, and future success.

Atomic Habits **by James Clear** — In this insightful book, James Clear reveals the science behind habit formation and offers practical strategies for building and sustaining positive habits. By understanding the psychology of behavior change, readers can learn how to make small, incremental changes that lead to significant improvements in their lives.

The Seven Habits of Highly Effective People **by Stephen R. Covey** — Covey presents a holistic approach to personal and professional development, outlining seven timeless principles for achieving success and fulfillment. Through anecdotes, insights, and practical exercises, Covey empowers readers to take control of their lives and become more effective leaders and individuals.

Website:

3DMoney.com

The 3D Money Solution — A unique five-step process that provides the tools needed to bring your money to life. Each step you take is designed to equip you with the tools and vision that will enable your money to work harder while providing you greater peace of mind in all areas of your life.

Videos:

Subscribe to our YouTube Channel 3D Money at:
Youtube.com/@3dmoney508

ABOUT THE AUTHORS

JEFF HUSTON

Jeff Huston is a business leader who understands the complex world of growing and protecting wealth. He is the chief visionary of the private investment group, 3D Money.

For 40 years, Jeff has owned and developed businesses. His Unique Ability is achieving growth-oriented excellence. He is all about the continual development and progression of leaders and influencers, elevating them to become the best version of themselves. He leads with authenticity and transparency and loves engaging with people who reciprocate.

Jeff is co-author of the Amazon bestselling book "Purpose, Passion, and Profit." He has won several National Achievement awards, has been a featured guest on many podcasts, and has presented at numerous national conventions.

Jeff is a Minnesota native, who resides in a small countryside community with his wife, Carol. Together they have two daughters and eight grandchildren.

GABE OLSON

Gabe Olson is an accomplished entrepreneur and leader. His primary role is visionary over multiple companies, including manufacturing, real estate, and agriculture. With an extensive background of over 15 years in the real estate business, project and property management, and construction.

Gabe and his wife, Andrea, co-authored a series of Amazon bestsellers teaching kids about prayer and how to look for God's miracles in everyday life. This is the heart of Gabe's work, and he is fueled every day by a deep sense of gratitude for what Christ has done. You can explore the series at www.thebiggodbooks.com.

Gabe is a Minnesota native and has been happily married to his wife, Andrea, for 18 years. Together, they have three daughters. He is a family man and is dedicated to being a great dad.

CONNECT WITH GABE

Follow him on Instagram today.

@gabeolsonofficial

CONNECT WITH

3D Money

Follow them on your favorite social media platforms today.

3DMoney.com

A FAITH-BASED ALTERNATIVE INVESTMENT COMPANY

3D Money

3D Money is a real estate investment company dedicated to searching out value-add, cash-flow opportunities in real property.

3DMoney.com

THIS BOOK IS PROTECTED INTELLECTUAL PROPERTY

The author of this book values Intellectual Property. The book you just read is protected by Easy IP®, a proprietary process, which integrates blockchain technology giving Intellectual Property "Global Protection." By creating a "Time-Stamped" smart contract that can never be tampered with or changed, we establish "First Use" that tracks back to the author.

Easy IP® functions much like a Pre-Patent™ since it provides an immutable "First Use" of the Intellectual Property. This is achieved through our proprietary process of leveraging blockchain technology and smart contracts. As a result, proving "First Use" is simple through a global and verifiable smart contract. By protecting intellectual property with blockchain technology and smart contracts, we establish a "First to File" event.

Protected By Easy IP®

LEARN MORE AT EASYIP.TODAY

www.ingramcontent.com/pod-product-compliance
Lightning Source LLC
Chambersburg PA
CBHW052149070526
44585CB00017B/2041